water

Technically Earth, Air, Fire and Water are not considered
elements in modern science. The Greeks included these
four as ''elements'' in their science because they believed
them to be the four basic qualities which made up all
substances.

Translation: W. Brian Altano

Pedagogical text: Cecilia Hernández de Lorenzo

First English language edition published 1985 by
Barron's Educational Series, Inc.

© Parramón Ediciones, S.A.
First Edition, September 1984
The title of the Spanish edition is *el agua*.

All inquiries should be addressed to:
Barron's Educational Series, Inc.
113 Crossways Park Drive
Woodbury, New York 11797

Library of Congress Catalog Card No. 85-6026

ISBN 0-8120-5744-9 (hardcover)
ISBN 0-8120-3599-2 (pbk.)

78   987654

Printed in Spain by Sirven Grafic, S.A.
Gran Vía, 754 - 08013 Barcelona
Legal Deposit: B-43.048-86

the four elements

water

Carme Solé Vendrell
J. M. Parramón

CHILDRENS PRESS CHOICE

A Barron's title selected for educational distribution

ISBN 0-516-08694-4

It's there, in the glass, to drink.

And it's there, in the pot, to boil...

...in the faucet, to wash...

in the watering can, to water...

...in the river to drink...

...in the canal...

...in the clouds...

It's there, in the fountain, to beautify...

and in the hose to put out the fire...

in the marsh, to create new life...

...and in the sea, to sail on.

Everywhere, to live!

IT'S WATER!

WATER

Water is the mother of life: in it we originated and evolved, protected from the adverse conditions in which the earth found itself in its beginnings.

The water that we drink

It is transparent, it has no smell, it has no flavor. If we try to catch it in our hands, it gets us wet, it escapes from us, it falls on the ground and leaves a puddle that disappears in a little while. Where does it go? Where does it come from?

The water cycle

You've seen rivers, lakes, and oceans. Water covers three quarters of our planet, and a large part of life develops in it.

With the warmth of the sun, it evaporates and rises, forming the clouds that you see in the sky. It stays there, as a vapor, floating in the air, until a cold stream condenses it and it falls in the form of rain, snow, or hail.

Most of this water falls on the sea, the rest on the land. The collision of water with the rocks wears them down, and little by little mountains are being rounded off. Water penetrates the soil, dissolving mineral substances that can be absorbed by plants. If the land is permeable, allowing the water to pass through, the water can sink to great depths, forming underground streams that later rise to the surface in the form of springs, rivers, or geysers.

Natural water

Look at a full glass of water against the light: you will see many particles floating. Natural water, from a spring or a river, is never pure. On its journey before rising to the surface and later in the riverbed, it dissolves different materials and drags along others that are not soluble.

We say that seawater is "salty" because it contains a lot of dissolved salt. The water in rivers and in the majority of lakes has little salt; this is "fresh" water. There are springs in which water mixes with gas: this is "mineral" water. Others, in which hot water flows, are "thermal" waters.

When you wash your hands, when you wash dishes or clothes, you are using water to lift some particles of dirt while dissolving other particles and rinsing them away.

Can water be cleaned?

The water that flows down the drain of the kitchen and bathroom sinks and the bathtub of your house circulates through small pipes until it reaches larger ones that take away all the wastes of an entire population.

If the population is small, these "residual" waters can be diverted to a river or the sea, where some microorganisms called bacteria decompose the waste and then purify it.

If the population is large or if the waters carry industrial wastes, it is necessary to purify them, because the bacteria are unable to handle the amount of wastes and the water would become contaminated.

Purifying plants clean fresh water. The first operation is a filtering process that catches large particles. The second phase is a chemical process called *flocculation*, which consists of adding substances that join with the small particles, making them easier to separate. Finally, the water is aerated by bacteria that finish eliminating the organic content.

If we want the resulting water to be "potable," that is to say that we can drink it without danger of infection, it must undergo a process of *chlorination.* Now you can drink it.

Are you thirsty?

On a summer day, when you have perspired a great deal, you are very thirsty. Did you remember to water the plants? Did you change the water for the canary? Water is indispensable for the maintenance of life. The food we eat is dissolved in water, then distributed inside our bodies. The waste products are expelled in perspiration and urine, also dissolved or suspended in water.

The mysteries of water

Aside from the great capacity to dissolve substances, water conceals other mysteries. It is capable of reflecting your face or a landscape as if it were a mirror. It can refract, or separate, light into seven colors of the rainbow, as if it were crystal.

If you leave a glass bottle full of water in the freezer through carelessness, you find it broken. This is due to the fact that water, upon solidifying, increases in volume, becoming ice. Ice is solid water and it floats on liquid water. Try it.

Let a pot full of water boil. You'll see that its content is decreasing, the water is being transformed into vapor. The vapor is very strong and is capable of raising the pot's lid and even of moving a train.

Water and people

We have learned many things about water. We have learned to channel it, to transport it, to move it, to recycle it, to store it in tanks and reservoirs (to use in periods of drought), to transform the power that it imposes on a turbine when it falls from the top of a dam into electricity...and many other things. It remains for us to solve two major problems related to water: its unequal distribution and the increase in contamination. The solution requires a great deal of international cooperation, since water is a common good that has no national boundaries.

The European Water Charter of 1968 sets forth the principles necessary for good administration of matters regarding water. It is a beginning in this cooperation. The U.S. Federal Water Pollution Control Act of 1972 was called the most comprehensive and powerful environmental law passed in our history. It sets high standards for water quality.

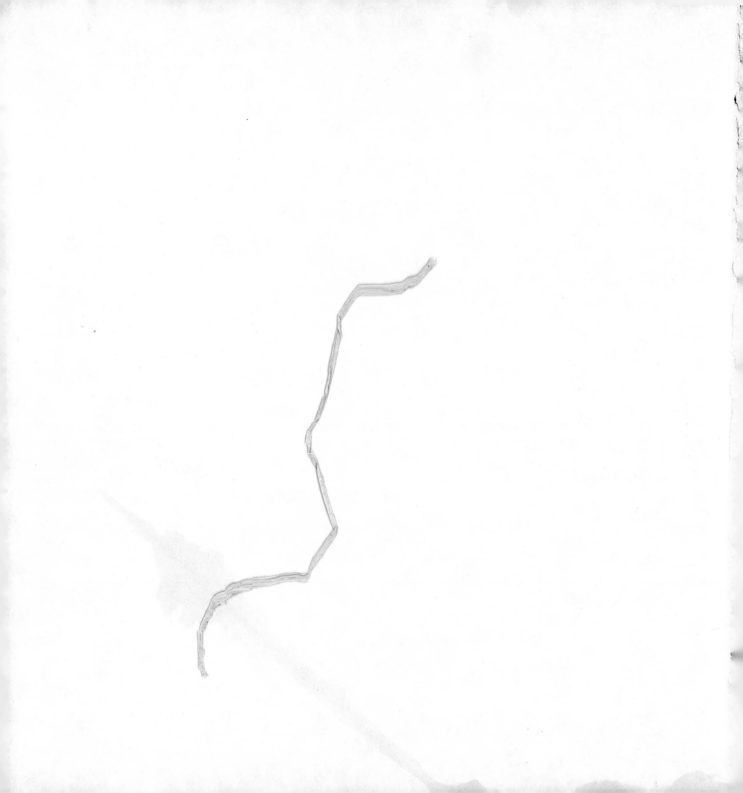